EYES WIDE OPEN

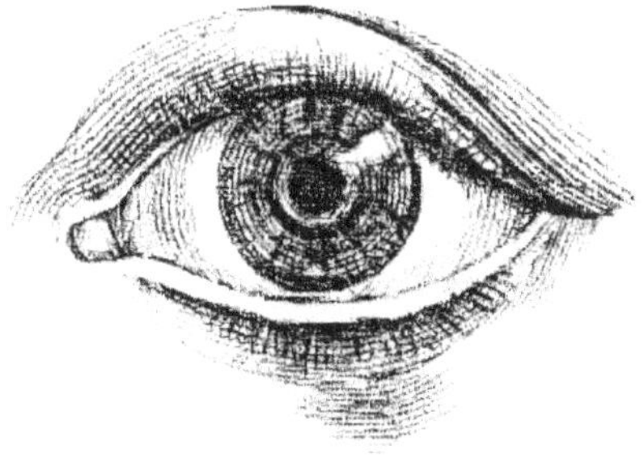

Addonis Willow

Table Of Contents

INTRODUCTION

Eyes Wide Open

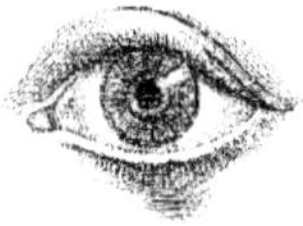

In a world marred by the pervasive presence of financial inequality, it is not just important but urgent for individuals to open their eyes and gain a deeper understanding of its profound impact on their lives. The purpose of this book goes beyond simply shedding light on the visible manifestations of financial inequality. It aims to unravel the complex web of its implications, exploring the hidden corners of our emotions, self-worth, aspirations, and relationships.

Economic disparity is not new; it has deep historical roots that continue to shape our present reality. Looking back, we can trace the origins of financial inequality to systems of power and exploitation that emerged as early as the agrarian age. The advent of capitalism further exacerbated these disparities, consolidating wealth and resources in the hands of the few while leaving the many struggling to survive.

The consequences of this inequality extend far beyond material wealth. It infiltrates every aspect of our lives, seeping into our emotional landscapes and shaping our self-perception. For those on the less privileged end of the spectrum, financial inequality can instill a deep sense of inadequacy and unworthiness. Society often equates wealth and success with personal value and achievement, fueling shame and self-doubt in those who fall short of societal expectations.

Financial dynamics bear the burden of structural inequality within relationships. Money has an astonishing power to shape interpersonal dynamics, often becoming a source of control, dependency, or resentment. The partner with more financial resources may wield their power to influence decisions, asserting control over significant life choices and creating an imbalance of power within the relationship. This power dynamic can lead to feelings of dependency or even inferiority, eroding trust and intimacy.

The impact of financial inequality also intertwines with the intersections of gender, race, and social class. Women, for example, continue to face significant disparities in pay and career opportunities, leading to a perpetuation of financial inequality. Similarly, racial and ethnic minorities find themselves disproportionately affected by systemic barriers that impede wealth accumulation and social mobility. By understanding these intersecting dimensions of inequality, we can better address the complex ways financial disparities are reinforced and sustained.

To truly comprehend and challenge financial inequality, we must shed our preconceived notions and interrogate the societal norms and constructs perpetuating these disparities. We must recognize the inherent privilege embedded within systems that advantage certain groups while marginalizing others and work towards dismantling these structures of oppression. By acknowledging our own biases and complicity in perpetuating inequality, and by fostering empathy and open communication, we can begin to actively participate in the pursuit of justice and equality for all.

Yet, navigating the complexities of financial inequality is not a task solely reliant on external actions. It requires a deeply introspective approach, as our internal landscapes are deeply and personally shaped by societal narratives and values surrounding wealth and success. By challenging and reevaluating our attitudes and beliefs about money, we can break free from the limitations imposed by financial inequality. We can redefine our understanding of wealth, shifting the narrative from material accumulation to personal fulfillment and contribution to the greater good.

This book seeks to empower readers with thought-provoking insights, practical advice, and inspiring stories, offering guidance on dismantling the barriers that restrict their financial well-being and hinder their ability to build fulfilling relationships. It calls on readers to question and challenge societal norms, reassess their values, and reshape their perceptions of wealth and worth. Together, we can pave the way for a future where financial equality is not just a distant dream but a tangible reality, creating a fairer and more compassionate world for all.

So let us embark on this journey, hand in hand, with our eyes wide open and hearts ready for transformation. Let us delve deep into financial inequality's historical, social, and emotional dimensions, unveiling the hidden complexities and demanding change. Together, we can confront financial inequality and forge a path toward a just and equitable world that values the inherent worth of every individual.

CHAPTER ONE

Acknowledging Financial Inequality

In today's society, it is impossible to ignore financial inequality's pervasive and alarming existence. The ever-widening gap between the rich and the poor has become an undeniable reality, and its far-reaching implications extend well beyond the superficial numbers that adorn a bank statement.

Truly acknowledging financial inequality is the crucial first step in understanding its profound impact on individuals, families, and entire communities. It demands a moral obligation to confront uncomfortable truths and bravely challenge the deeply ingrained beliefs and systemic structures perpetuating this alarming disparity.

Indeed, one of the greatest impediments to acknowledging financial inequality is the prevailing tendency to view it through the narrow prism of personal responsibility. Society often attributes financial success or failure solely to individual choices and actions, inadvertently neglecting the critical examination of systemic factors contributing to this deeply woven social issue. These systemic factors include but are not limited to, unequal access to quality education, discriminatory hiring practices, and the perpetuation of wealth within certain social circles.

However, it is vital to recognize that financial inequality does not simply result from personal shortcomings or failures. Instead, it is deeply rooted in longstanding systemic biases, discriminatory practices, and unequal opportunities that have systematically shaped our economic landscape.

Historically, our societies have been structured to disproportionately favor certain segments of the population while leaving others at a significant disadvantage. These disparities can be traced back to historical factors such as colonization, slavery, and discriminatory laws that have created entrenched patterns of wealth accumulation and exclusion.

Within this unequal framework, numerous factors perpetuate and amplify financial inequality. Education plays a pivotal role, as access to quality education and the opportunities it provides become a decisive factor in an individual's economic prospects. Unfortunately, disadvantaged communities often face underfunded schools and limited access to educational resources, leading to diminished opportunities for upward mobility.

Discrimination also significantly contributes to financial inequality. Women, for example, continue to face disparities in wages, often earning less than their male counterparts for the same work. Similarly, people of color encounter systemic barriers that limit their access to well-paying jobs and inhibit social mobility. Discrimination is not only limited to these groups; individuals with disabilities, members of the LGBTQ+ community, and other marginalized groups also face unique challenges in attaining financial stability.

Financial inequality introduces complex dynamics within relationships that can strain even the strongest foundations. When one partner possesses significantly more financial resources than the other, it can breed feelings of inadequacy, dependency, and resentment. Power imbalances can emerge, impacting decision-making within the household and reinforcing traditional gender roles.

Moreover, financial inequality significantly influences decisions about shared responsibilities, such as household expenses, healthcare, and childcare. In situations where one partner earns significantly less, it can lead to feelings of guilt or a loss of agency. This creates additional challenges when it comes to decisions involving long-term financial planning, major purchases, and investments for the future.

Understanding and acknowledging financial inequality is the preliminary step towards addressing it and striving for change. This necessitates a collective effort to challenge the conventional notions of success and value perpetuating current affairs. In doing so, we must advocate for the creation of more equitable economic systems, break down the barriers that obstruct marginalized groups from accessing resources and opportunities, and dismantle the systemic injustices that perpetuate financial inequality.

Truly acknowledging financial inequality also emphasizes the importance of cultivating empathy, compassion, and understanding. Merely acknowledging its existence is insufficient; we must actively engage in meaningful actions to create a society that affords everyone equal opportunities and unhindered access to essential resources.

The subsequent chapters explore financial inequality's profound and multifaceted impacts on relationships, the importance of open and honest communication about money matters, and practical strategies for building financial independence. By diving deeper into these crucial topics, we hope to provide a comprehensive guide for navigating the complexities of financial inequality. Ultimately, we aim to empower individuals and communities to create a more equitable, inclusive, and fulfilling future for themselves, their loved ones, and society.

CHAPTER TWO

Understanding Your Worth Beyond Finances

In a society that often measures success and worth based on financial status, it can be easy to get caught up in believing that your bank account solely determines your value. However, it is crucial to understand that your worth extends far beyond monetary possessions.

When we talk about worth beyond nances, we refer to each individual's intrinsic value. It goes beyond the materialistic notions of success and delves into what makes us human. It encompasses the intangible qualities and experiences that shape our identity and contribute to our well-being.

To truly understand your worth, you must first recognize your strengths and embrace the qualities that make you who you are. Take the time to reflect on your accomplishments, both big and small. Celebrate the moments where you challenged yourself, overcame obstacles, and persevered. These moments are not simply achievements to be checked off a list but are testaments to your determination, resilience, and personal growth.

Beyond external accomplishments, your worth lies in the values that guide your actions and interactions with others. It is in the kindness, empathy, and compassion you extend to those around you. It is the ability to make someone feel seen, heard, and understood. Your worth is amplified through the connections you make, the positive impact you have within your community, and the difference you make in the lives of others.

Understanding your worth beyond nances also means acknowledging your character's and integrity's impact. It is about being true to yourself, holding onto your principles, and standing up for what you believe in, even in the face of adversity. This unwavering commitment to your values allows you to live a life aligned with your authentic self, leading to greater fulfillment and inner peace.

Furthermore, your worth extends to the relationships you cultivate and nurture. Your ability to love, support, and be present for others is a testament to your emotional intelligence and your capacity for empathy. It is in the laughter shared with friends, the comfort provided to a loved one in times of need, and the genuine connections formed that you find your true worth. These relationships, built on trust, respect, and reciprocity, enrich your life and contribute to your well-being.

Temporary setbacks or perceived failures do not diminish your worth. Instead, these experiences offer valuable lessons and opportunities for growth. They test your resilience, push you to reflect, and inspire personal transformation. Embracing these moments as part of your journey allows you to learn from them, adapt, and continue moving forward with grace and strength.

It is essential to recognize that financial success may provide comfort and security, but it should not be the sole determinant of your self-worth. Your worth is not tied to your material possessions or your bank balance. Instead, focus on cultivating a sense of worth grounded in self-acceptance and self-love. Embrace and appreciate your unique qualities, passions, and talents.

Understanding your worth beyond nances also means resisting the temptation of comparison. Each person's journey and circumstances are unique, and focusing on your path and personal growth is essential instead of measuring yourself against others. Celebrate their successes without undermining your own. Remember that we all have different definitions of success and that true worth is not a competition but a realization of our potential.

You empower yourself with genuine self-confidence and contentment by embracing your worth beyond nances. You can strive towards personal and professional goals driven by purpose and passion rather than a need to accumulate wealth solely. This perspective allows you to maintain a healthy relationship with money, viewing it as a tool to support your overall well-being and happiness rather than as the sole measure of success.

In conclusion, when understanding your worth beyond nances, it is essential to recognize and appreciate your unique qualities, your positive impact on others, and the value you bring to the world. By grounding your sense of worth in these intrinsic qualities, you can build a strong foundation for personal growth, contentment, and fulfillment, regardless of your financial circumstances.

Remember, your worth goes beyond the digits in your bank account. It reflects your character, the relationships you build, the positive changes you make in the world, and the deep connection you have with your authentic self. Embrace your worth, cherish it, and let it guide you towards a life of purpose and fulfillment.

CHAPTER THREE

The Impact Of Financial Inequality On Relationships

Financial inequality can profoundly and multifacetedly impact relationships, permeating every aspect of a partnership and potentially contributing to long-term detrimental effects. When one partner earns significantly more than the other, it can create a power disparity, influencing how money is managed and the overall dynamics between partners.

One core challenge of financial inequality is the discrepancy in lifestyle choices and spending habits. The partner who earns more may have access to lavish luxuries while the other struggles to make ends meet. This stark contrast in financial circumstances can breed feelings of inadequacy, jealousy, and resentment. The partner with limited financial means may constantly question their worth, feeling they cannot contribute equally or keep up with their wealthier counterpart. Over time, this can erode the foundation of trust and equality within the relationship.

Furthermore, financial inequality can significantly impact the division of household responsibilities. In many cases, the partner who earns less or not at all may assume a greater share of domestic duties, compensating for their perceived lower financial contribution. This dynamic, though understandable on the surface, can lead to an imbalance of financial and emotional labor within the relationship. The partner who earns less may feel overwhelmed by the disproportionate burden they shoulder, resulting in feelings of resentment and frustration.

Financial inequality can also influence decision-making within the relationship. The partner with a higher income may be deemed the primary authority in economic matters, potentially leaving the other partner with a diminished sense of autonomy and decision-making power. This power imbalance can undermine open communication and erode trust, hindering the relationship's overall health.

Moreover, financial inequality can amplify societal inequalities, such as gender dynamics and social class divisions. Traditional gender roles and expectations often dictate that men should be the primary breadwinners, while women may carry the burden of managing the household and childcare responsibilities. These predefined roles can become deeply entrenched, affecting not only the couple's allocation of financial resources but also their perceptions of self-worth and societal status.

The power dynamics can be complex and pose substantial challenges for couples with whom one partner has significantly more wealth or income. The partner with more financial resources may hold disproportionate decision-making power, leading to feelings of disempowerment and voicelessness for the other partner. Moreover, societal expectations and norms may pressure the lower-earning partner to conform to the desires and preferences of the wealthier counterpart, further exacerbating the power imbalance and eroding their sense of autonomy and agency.

To address the impact of financial inequality on relationships, couples must engage in open and honest conversations that seek to explore and understand each other's perspectives, concerns, and expectations. These conversations should foster empathy, emphasizing mutual respect and the importance of equitable decision-making.

It is incumbent upon the partner with the higher income to acknowledge and sympathize with the financial struggles of their counterpart. This may necessitate a willingness to adjust spending habits, evaluate shared financial goals, and find ways to support the other partner's financial independence and career growth. By actively involving both partners in financial decision-making, a sense of shared responsibility, and empowerment can be fostered.

Creating a joint budget becomes imperative to bridge the financial gap and align priorities within the relationship. Developing a transparent financial plan that considers both partners' needs, desires, and financial capabilities can promote a more harmonious and balanced approach to money management. It also allows both partners to contribute their unique perspectives and expertise.

Addressing the impact of financial inequality requires ongoing dedication and effort from both partners. Establishing a foundation of open and honest communication built on empathy and understanding is crucial. Regular check-ins, subsequent adjustments to financial practices, and a shared vision for financial security and equality can help a couple navigate the challenges successfully and build a stronger, more resilient partnership.

By actively challenging societal norms and expectations surrounding financial inequality, couples can work to create a relationship that transcends monetary limitations and allows for the n ourishing of both partners. Recognizing the inherent value of each individual's contribution beyond the realm of nances fosters an environment of mutual support and respect. Celebrating both partners' non-monetary qualities and strengths can help redefine success and happiness within the relationship. Together, couples can navigate the complexities of financial inequality and build a partnership grounded in love, equality, and shared aspirations.

CHAPTER FOUR

Communicating With Your Partner About Money

Money is often considered taboo in relationships, but open and honest communication about finances is essential for a strong and prosperous partnership.

Although discussing money can be uncomfortable and may lead to conflicts, avoiding these conversations can create misunderstandings, breed resentment, and even cause financial strain. Therefore, prioritizing discussions about nances is crucial for building a healthy and successful future together.

Initiating a conversation about money requires creating a safe and non-judgmental environment. Choose a time when you and your partner are calm and receptive, ideally free from distractions. Begin by expressing your genuine desire to have an open and transparent discussion about nances, framing it as an opportunity to work together as a team and achieve mutual goals. Highlight that this conversation is not intended to assign blame or criticize each other's financial decisions but to foster understanding, cooperation, and shared responsibilities.

When broaching the topic, sharing your feelings and thoughts about money can be helpful. Discuss how your upbringing has influenced your attitudes and behaviors towards nances. Be open and vulnerable about money-related fears or anxieties, acknowledging that these emotions may impact your decision-making process. Encourage your partner to do the same, creating a space where you can discuss your financial histories and insecurities. This level of vulnerability fosters camaraderie and empathy, allowing both individuals to gain a deeper understanding of each other's perspectives and experiences.

Moving forward, it is crucial to discuss your individual

financial goals. Take the time to outline your short-term and long-term objectives clearly. Share your debts and financial obligations, as well as how you prioritize saving and spending. Consider discussing your career aspirations, desired lifestyle, and retirement plans for a comprehensive understanding. In turn, encourage your partner to express their goals and dreams. By opening up about your financial ambitions, you gain insight into each other's priorities and values, enabling you to find common ground and develop a joint plan that aligns with your hopes and dreams.

Establishing financial boundaries is another vital aspect of these conversations. By agreeing on how decisions will be made regarding money, you set the stage for a smoother financial journey. Discuss how you will handle joint expenses, such as bills or household and individual expenses. Decide whether you will maintain separate bank accounts or combine your nances. Additionally, address how you will handle unexpected expenses or financial emergencies. Moreover, laying out a framework for making decisions about larger purchases or investments is essential, ensuring that both partners have equal input.

Setting clear guidelines in these areas helps avoid misunderstandings and fosters a sense of fairness, equality, and trust in your financial partnership.

Remember that regular check-ins are crucial for maintaining healthy communication about money. Schedule regular meetings to review your budget, assess your progress towards financial goals, and address any concerns or changes in circumstances. This ongoing dialogue provides an opportunity to reevaluate and adjust your financial plans as needed, demonstrating your commitment to actively working together towards financial stability and prosperity.

It is crucial to recognize that effective communication about money extends beyond discussing numbers and budgets. Active listening, respect, and a willingness to compromise are vital components of these conversations. Be open to your partner's perspectives, understanding that their experiences and values may differ from your own. Encourage them to express their thoughts and feelings, ensuring that their voice is heard and valued. Remember that compromise often plays a significant role in f i nding solutions that accommodate both partners' needs and aspirations. By fostering a supportive and respectful environment, you create a strong foundation for navigating financial challenges and successes as a team.

Another important aspect of financial conversations is exploring how money influences your emotional and psychological well-being. Money can evoke strong feelings and trigger personal insecurities, so it is essential to be aware of how these emotions manifest in yourself and your partner. Encourage open discussions about money-related stress, fears, and anxieties, creating a safe space to share without judgement. By understanding the emotional aspects tied to money, you can better support and empathize with one another, fostering a deeper emotional bond.

In addition to discussing financial goals, boundaries, and emotions, it is helpful to establish a system for tracking and managing your nances. Consider creating a shared budget, tracking expenses, and setting financial targets together. This collaborative approach promotes transparency and accountability while fostering shared responsibility. It is also essential to address any discrepancies in income or financial contributions, ensuring that both partners feel valued and respected for their contributions to the relationship.

It is worth mentioning that external influences, such as cultural backgrounds and societal expectations, can significantly impact our attitudes towards money. Engage in open and respectful conversations about how your cultural backgrounds shape your financial perspectives. By understanding each other's cultural beliefs and values, you can find ways to navigate potential conflicts or differences that may arise due to divergent financial attitudes. For instance, if one partner values saving for the future while the other prefers to enjoy the present, finding a balance between these two perspectives can be a point of compromise.

You can strengthen your relationship and build a solid foundation for financial stability and success by engaging in open and honest conversations about money. Embrace these conversations as opportunities for growth, understanding, and shared responsibility.

Remember, effective communication about money requires ongoing commitment and a willingness to adapt as circumstances evolve. Together, you and your partner can navigate the complexities of money, fostering trust, security, and mutual support every step of the way.

CHAPTER FIVE

Setting Financial Goals As A Couple

In any relationship, it is important for partners to align their financial goals and work together towards achieving them. This becomes even more crucial in cases where there is financial inequality between partners. Setting financial goals as a couple not only helps in creating a sense of unity and purpose but also ensures that both individuals are actively involved in decision-making and have a stake in their financial future.

The first step in setting financial goals together is to have open and honest communication. This involves more than just discussing numbers and figures; it requires a deeper understanding of each other's values, beliefs, and attitudes towards money. Each partner should express their individual financial aspirations, concerns, and priorities.

When partners engage in open and honest communication, they create a safe space where they can share their dreams and fears regarding money. This shared vulnerability fosters trust and strengthens the bond between partners. It allows them to uncover any underlying beliefs or behaviors related to money that may affect their financial goals.

In these discussions, it is important to approach the topic of money with sensitivity and respect. Money is often associated with emotions such as security, stability, and control. Partners should create a safe space where they can openly express their financial vulnerabilities, without fear of judgment or criticism.

Building a foundation of trust and mutual understanding allows couples to navigate financial inequality and establish a joint vision for their future. It is essential to recognize that financial inequality can arise from a variety of factors such as income disparities, student loans, or past financial obligations. By openly discussing these aspects, couples can identify ways to bridge the gap and work together towards their shared financial goals.

Once individual goals have been discussed, it is essential to identify shared goals as a couple. These are financial objectives that both partners agree on and are invested in achieving. It could be paying oL debt, saving for a child's education, or increasing their retirement savings.

Shared goals help in fostering teamwork and mutual support, as each partner actively contributes and participates in decision-making. They create a sense of unity and shared responsibility, increasing the chances of successfully achieving financial milestones. Partners should take the time to ensure that the shared goals they set align with their shared values and aspirations. This shared vision becomes the driving force behind their financial journey, leading to a sense of accomplishment and motivation when milestones are reached.

When setting financial goals, it is important to ensure that they are specific, measurable, attainable, relevant, and time-bound (SMART). This means that goals should be clearly defined, quantifiable, realistic, relevant to the couple's circumstances, and have a timeline attached to them.

Specific goals provide clarity and direction, aiding in effective decision-making and resource allocation. Measurable goals allow couples to track their progress and celebrate small victories along the way. For instance, reaching a certain savings target could be celebrated with a special dinner or a small trip. Attainable goals help in maintaining motivation and avoiding discouragement. Relevant goals ensure that the couple's aspirations are aligned with their current life stage and financial situation. Lastly, time-bound goals create a sense of urgency and help in prioritizing efforts.

Setting SMART goals helps in maintaining focus, tracking progress, and celebrating achievements along the way. Without such clarity, couples may face challenges in achieving their desired outcomes, leading to frustration and potential strain on the relationship.

In cases of financial inequality, it is crucial to consider and respect each partner's financial contributions and limitations. This means that goals should be set in a way that is fair and attainable for both partners. If one partner earns significantly more than the other, it may be important to establish goals that take into account this discrepancy, ensuring that both individuals feel valued and heard.

Financial inequality should not be seen as a source of power imbalance or resentment. Instead, it should be viewed as an opportunity for growth, understanding, and achieving mutual financial success. Collaboratively setting goals that consider individual circumstances and limitations promotes a sense of fairness and equality within the relationship.

Another aspect to consider when setting financial goals as a couple is the need for flexibility. Life is full of uncertainties, and circumstances may change unexpectedly. Unexpected expenses, job transitions, or shifts in financial priorities may require adjustments to the original goals.

It is important to revisit and adjust goals periodically, allowing for adaptability and ensuring they remain relevant to the couple's evolving financial situation. By regularly evaluating their goals, couples can proactively address challenges, seize opportunities, and realign their efforts to stay on track.

Flexibility also fosters open communication and reinforces the importance of working together towards a common vision. It encourages couples to think creatively and explore new possibilities when faced with obstacles.

Couples can create a joint budget to effectively work towards their financial goals. A joint budget not only helps in tracking expenses, managing income, and allocating funds towards different goals, but it also promotes transparency and shared responsibility.

Budgeting as a couple requires a collaborative effort. Each partner should actively participate and contribute to the budgeting process, ensuring that both individuals have a say in financial decisions. By involving both partners, a joint budget becomes a tool for shared financial growth and accountability.

When creating a joint budget, it is important to strike a balance between individual wants and needs. Collaborative decision-making ensures that both partners feel heard, understood, and supported. Establishing guidelines or rules that govern how money is allocated within the budget may be helpful, promoting fairness and minimizing conflicts.

Regularly reviewing the budget together enables partners to stay on track and make necessary adjustments to ensure progress towards their goals. It also provides an opportunity to assess spending patterns, identify areas for adjustment, and celebrate milestones achieved.

In addition to goal-setting and budgeting, couples should prioritize building an emergency fund. Life is unpredictable, and having a financial safety net is essential to navigating unexpected situations or emergencies.

Creating an emergency fund should be a joint effort, regardless of income disparities. By setting aside a portion of their income into a dedicated emergency fund, couples can ensure they are prepared for unforeseen events without derailing their long-term financial objectives.

An emergency fund provides a sense of security and reduces financial stress within the relationship. It cushions during challenging times, preventing the need to rely on credit cards or loans that can lead to further financial strain.

Lastly, setting financial goals as a couple involves celebrating achievements and milestones, whether big or small. Recognizing and rewarding progress helps maintain motivation and foster a sense of accomplishment.

Couples should celebrate their achievements in a meaningful way that aligns with their shared values. It is an opportunity to reflect on their progress together and reaffirm their commitment to their financial journey. Celebrations can range from a simple acknowledgment to a small treat or experience reinforcing the couple's commitment to their shared financial journey.

In conclusion, setting financial goals as a couple is a multifaceted process beyond just numbers. It requires open and honest communication, empathy, and the creation of a shared vision. By engaging in open dialogue, recognizing individual and shared goals, setting SMART objectives, considering individual contributions and limitations, remaining flexible, creating a joint budget, building an emergency fund, and celebrating achievements, couples can work towards financial empowerment, resilience, and a secure future together.

CHAPTER SIX

Creating A Budget That Reflects Your Realities

Creating a budget is an essential step towards financial stability and success, especially when dealing with financial inequality within a relationship. When your income and financial responsibilities differ from your partner's, it becomes crucial to develop a budget that takes both of your realities into account. You can create a budget that promotes open communication, fairness, and a shared financial vision by carefully considering your unique circumstances.

To begin, start by reviewing your individual incomes,

expenditures, and financial goals. Take into account your personal expenses such as rent or mortgage payments, utilities, groceries, transportation, insurance, healthcare, and any personal debts or obligations. Similarly, do this exercise with your partner, ensuring that transparency prevails throughout the process.

Understanding and acknowledging the financial inequality within a relationship is essential. It can arise due to differences in income, educational opportunities, career paths, or previous financial responsibilities. By acknowledging these disparities, you can approach the budgeting process with empathy and understanding, allowing for a more collaborative and fair approach.

Once you have an overview of each other's financial obligations, it's time to merge your budgets. This may seem daunting at first, but creating a comprehensive plan that accounts for both partners' financial situations is essential.

Begin by categorizing your joint expenses, such as shared bills, groceries, and vacations. It is crucial to determine how these expenses will be divided equally or proportionately based on each person's income. Open and honest communication is key during this process, as it can help identify potential concerns or challenges.

When financial inequality exists in a relationship, it is important to address it in a way that fosters understanding and fairness. Consider adopting a proportional approach to dividing joint expenses. This means each partner contributes a percentage of their income towards shared expenses, reflecting their respective financial realities. For example, if one partner earns 60% of the total household income, they would contribute 60% towards joint expenses, while the other contributes 40%.

However, it is essential to remember that financial responsibility is not solely based on income. Other factors, such as student loan debt, childcare expenses, or supporting family members, may impact the ability to contribute towards joint expenses. In these cases, it is crucial to approach the budgeting process with empathy and f l exibility.

When setting financial goals, it is crucial to consider the challenges and obstacles that financial inequality may pose. For example, if one partner has significant student loan debt, it may impact their ability to contribute towards joint savings. In such cases, it's essential to be understanding and flexible, finding alternative ways to support each other without causing additional financial stress.

Additionally, prioritize having open and honest conversations about financial goals and aspirations. Discuss your short-term and long-term financial objectives as a couple, whether saving for a home, planning for retirement, or investing in further education. By aligning your financial goals, you can work towards them and support each other.

It's important to understand that a budget should not only involve dividing expenses but also involve setting financial goals together. By sharing your dreams and aspirations, you can motivate and support each other in achieving them. This approach fosters a sense of teamwork and unity, allowing you to face financial challenges together.

As you finalize your budget, it's crucial to revisit and evaluate it periodically. Life circumstances can change, and it's vital to ensure your budget continues to reflect your realities and aspirations. Regularly review your income, expenses, and goals, and make any necessary adjustments together.

Remember, a budget is meant to provide structure and clarity, not to restrict or create tension within your relationship. It is a tool that empowers both partners and promotes financial harmony. Be flexible and open-minded as you navigate the process together. Appreciate that compromise and mutual understanding are crucial to creating a budget reflecting your realities.

By working together to create a budget that incorporates both partners' financial situations, you can strengthen your relationship and build a solid foundation for your shared future. Keeping your eyes wide open to the reality of financial inequality and approaching it with empathy and understanding will lead to a happier, more equitable, and prosperous life as a couple.

CHAPTER SEVEN

Navigating Power Dynamics In A Financially Unequal Marriage

In a financially unequal marriage, power dynamics can become a significant source of tension and conflict if not addressed and managed effectively. The dynamics of power typically arise when one partner has a higher income or greater financial resources compared to the other. However, it is crucial to recognize that power imbalances can exist even in relationships where both partners contribute financially, as it goes beyond income and encompasses control, decision-making, and societal expectations.

Financial inequality within a marriage can arise due to various reasons, such as differences in education, career choices, or personal circumstances. When one partner has a higher income, it can lead to disparities in decision-making power, influence over financial matters, and societal perceptions. If not addressed, these imbalances can be internalized and impact self-esteem, sense of worth, and overall relationship dynamics.

One of the first steps in navigating power dynamics is establishing a foundation of open and honest communication. This means creating a safe space where both partners can express their thoughts, concerns, and aspirations without fear of judgment. Regular check-ins to discuss financial matters, goals, and any challenges can help foster trust and maintain open lines of communication, ensuring that neither partner feels left out or powerless.

To foster equality and respect, it is essential to understand that financial inequality does not equate to a lack of value or worth within the relationship. Both partners should be regarded as equals, recognizing that contributions extend beyond monetary means.

Acknowledging and appreciating non-financial contributions, such as emotional support, caregiving responsibilities, and personal growth, can help balance power dynamics and promote overall well-being within the relationship.

However, despite the importance of non-financial contributions, it is crucial to address financial imbalances' influence on decision-making and individual autonomy. The partner with greater financial resources may unintentionally exert more control over choices related to household expenses, investments, and major purchases. This dynamic could create a sense of powerlessness for the partner with lower income, leading to feelings of resentment or diminished independence.

In navigating power imbalances, it is crucial to establish a system of decision-making that genuinely considers both partners' perspectives. Recognizing individual strengths and expertise in different areas of life can help distribute decision-making power more equitably. It is essential to create a space for compromise and collaboration when it comes to financial decisions. This may involve finding a balance between individual financial autonomy and shared decision-making based on the couple's specific circumstances.

Developing a budgeting process that considers both partners' financial contributions, goals, and aspirations can help alleviate power imbalances and promote a sense of fairness. Both partners should have an equal say in setting financial goals, discussing priorities, and determining spending limits. An open and ongoing dialogue about financial expectations, budgeting strategies, and long-term plans can foster a greater sense of partnership and reduce the potential for power struggles.

Challenging traditional gender roles and expectations can also be necessary to address power dynamics in a financially unequal marriage. Societal norms often dictate that the higher earner has more control or influence over financial matters. However, it is vital to question these expectations and seek alternative arrangements that suit both partners' needs and aspirations. Redefining roles within the relationship and sharing financial and non-financial responsibilities can help distribute power more evenly and promote a sense of equality.

Both partners should actively engage in self-rea ction to evaluate their beliefs, biases, and assumptions about money, gender, and power. Questioning societal narratives and challenging personal attitudes can lead to a shift in perspectives, allowing for greater empathy and understanding. By recognizing and addressing their biases, partners can create a space for open and meaningful discussions that transcend societal expectations.

Addressing power dynamics also necessitates empathy and understanding. It is crucial to put oneself in the other person's shoes and consider the emotions and challenges they may be experiencing. By practicing empathy, each partner can gain a deeper understanding of the other's perspective, leading to greater compassion and cooperation. This understanding extends beyond financial matters and encompasses emotional needs, personal aspirations, and the desire for individual growth.

In some instances, seeking professional help, such as couples therapy or financial counseling, can be highly beneficial in navigating power dynamics in a financially unequal marriage.

Trained professionals can guide both partners through discussions, offer strategies for effective communication and decision-making, and provide valuable insights into managing power imbalances. Professional guidance can be beneficial for addressing deep-rooted beliefs, healing emotional wounds, and fostering a stronger and more equitable relationship.

Navigating power dynamics in a financially unequal

marriage requires a commitment to open communication, mutual respect, compromise, and occasional outside support. It is important to remember that the value of a relationship lies in the strength of the partnership, shared values, and the love and support provided rather than in financial means alone. By actively addressing power imbalances, couples can work towards a more equitable and fulfilling relationship where both partners feel valued, heard, and empowered.

CHAPTER EIGHT

Building Your Financial Independence

In a world of financial inequality, achieving financial independence becomes increasingly essential. It empowers individuals to control their financial future and make decisions that align with their goals and values. This chapter delves deeper into strategies and steps to help you navigate and build your path toward financial independence.

1. Assess Your Current Financial Situation:

Take a detailed assessment of your current financial status to understand your position clearly. This evaluation should include analyzing your income, expenses, assets, liabilities, financial habits, and behaviors.

Understanding your relationship with money, including spending patterns, saving, and investing, is vital to identifying areas for improvement. By identifying potential pitfalls and areas of growth, you can establish a baseline from which to develop your financial plan.

2. Set Realistic Goals:

Determining your financial goals is a crucial part of achieving independence. While it is essential to dream big, setting realistic and achievable targets will provide you with a roadmap for success. Start by identifying short-term, medium-term, and long-term goals and break them down into specific, measurable, attainable, relevant, and time-bound (SMART) objectives. Whether it's paying off debt, saving for retirement, starting a business, or purchasing a home, clearly define your goals, outline the necessary steps to achieve them, and continually reassess and adjust as needed.

3. Create a Comprehensive Budget:

Budgeting is a fundamental tool for managing your finances and working towards independence. Start by identifying your essential expenses, such as housing, utilities, transportation, and food. Allocate a portion of your income towards savings and investments to ensure future financial security. Carefully evaluate discretionary spending categories, such as entertainment, dining out, vacations, and areas where you can reduce or eliminate unnecessary costs. Regularly track your expenses using budgeting tools or apps, and make conscious spending decisions to align your expenditures with your financial goals.

4. Increase Your Income:

While managing expenses is crucial, increasing your income can significantly boost your journey towards financial independence. Consider exploring alternative sources of income such as freelancing, starting a side business or gig, investing in income-generating assets, or even upskilling to secure a higher-paying job. Diversifying your income streams provides additional financial security and flexibility, allowing you to allocate more towards savings, investments, debt repayment, and personal growth.

5. Develop Strong Financial Literacy:

Educating yourself about personal finance is crucial for achieving and maintaining financial independence. Take the time to read books, attend seminars, or participate in online courses focusing on budgeting, investing, debt management, and long-term financial planning. Arm yourself with knowledge and empower yourself to make informed decisions that align with your aspirations. Additionally, stay updated on current financial news, trends, and economic indicators to make informed investment decisions and navigate market fluctuations.

6. Build an Emergency Fund:

Creating an emergency fund should be a top priority as you work towards financial independence. Set aside a portion of your income in a separate, easily accessible account to cover unexpected expenses or financial setbacks. Having an emergency fund will provide you with peace of mind and ensure that you don't have to rely on credit or jeopardize your progress toward financial freedom. Aim to save three to six months' worth of expenses in this fund for a strong safety net.

7. Pay OL Debt:

Debt can impede your ability to achieve financial independence. Develop a systematic plan to pay all high-interest debts, starting with those with the highest interest rates. Devote a portion of your budget towards debt repayment through the snowball method (starting with the smallest debt) or the avalanche method (starting with the highest interest rate debt). Prioritize paying all credit card debt, student loans, and any other outstanding loans to free up your income and accelerate your progress towards financial freedom.

8. Invest for the Future:

Investing is critical to building long-term wealth and financial independence. Consult a reputable financial advisor or educate yourself about investment options, risk tolerance, and diversification strategies. Understand the power of compound interest and the benefits of investing in various asset classes, such as stocks, bonds, mutual funds, real estate, or retirement accounts. Regularly contribute to your investments, automate your savings, and stay updated on market trends to maximize your returns and build a robust portfolio over time.

9. Continuously Reassess and Adjust:

Financial independence is not a one-time achievement but rather an ongoing journey.

Review your financial plan regularly to assess its effectiveness and make necessary adjustments. Life circumstances, economic conditions, and personal goals may change, so your plan should be flexible and adaptable. Monitor your progress, celebrate milestones, and recalibrate your strategy to ensure your financial plan always aligns with your current situation and future aspirations.

10. Protect Your Financial Independence:

As you attain financial independence, it becomes crucial to protect the progress you've made. Consider measures such as having adequate insurance coverage, safeguarding assets, and establishing an estate plan. Insurance policies, such as health, life, property, and liability insurance, protect against unexpected events that could derail your financial stability. Properly managing, preserving, and passing on your assets through estate planning ensures your hard-earned wealth is passed on to future generations or utilized according to your wishes.

11. Cultivate a Wealth Mindset:

Achieving financial independence also requires developing a wealth mindset. This mindset involves a shift in how you think about money, abundance, and your ability to create wealth. Embrace an abundance mindset by focusing on opportunities, growth, and gratitude rather than scarcity or limitations. Surround yourself with like-minded individuals who share your financial aspirations and can provide support, guidance, and motivation. Continuously grow your financial education and remain open to new ideas, perspectives, and strategies that can accelerate your path toward financial independence.

Building financial independence requires discipline, resilience, and a long-term mindset. It will have its challenges and triumphs along the way. By taking proactive steps, setting realistic goals, continuously educating yourself, and cultivating a wealth mindset, you can gradually break free from financial inequality and create a life of financial stability, autonomy, and abundance. Enjoy the journey towards financial independence, embracing it with confidence and determination, as it leads you towards a brighter and more secure future.

CHAPTER NINE

Planning For The Future: Investments, Retirement, And Estate Planning

As individuals and couples, it is essential to plan for the future regarding financial stability and ensure our loved ones are taken care of in our absence. This chapter delves into the crucial aspects of investments, retirement planning, and estate planning, providing readers with invaluable insights and guidance.

Investments play a pivotal role in securing a financially stable and prosperous future. They serve as a means to grow wealth and protect against inflation. Understanding the basics of investing is essential, regardless of whether you're a novice or an experienced investor. This chapter dives deeper into different investment avenues, highlighting their characteristics, risks, and potential returns.

Stocks, being equities, represent ownership in a company. They offer the potential for high returns but also come with higher risks. This chapter explores different types of stocks - common and preferred - and provides insights on assessing their value, understanding stock market fluctuations, and the importance of diversification to reduce risk.

In addition to standard and preferred stocks, this chapter delves further into other investment options within the equity market. It discusses concepts such as exchange-traded funds (ETFs), which provide diversification across multiple stocks or industries, and dividend stocks, which offer regular income streams. It explores the benefits and risks associated with sector, growth, value, and income investing, enabling readers to make strategic investment decisions aligned with their financial goals and risk tolerance.

On the other hand, bonds provide fixed income and are considered a safer investment option. This chapter delves into the various types of bonds, including government, corporate, municipal, and international bonds. It discusses the factors influencing bond prices, such as interest rates and credit ratings, enabling readers to make informed decisions when including bonds in their investment portfolio.

Furthermore, this chapter explains the concept of bond laddering—an investment strategy that involves owning a mix of bonds with staggered maturity dates—to help manage interest rate risk and maximize potential returns. It also explores the possible benefits and risks of investing in inflation-linked, convertible, and high-yield bonds, providing readers with a comprehensive understanding of the bond market.

Mutual funds are another popular investment avenue that pools funds from multiple investors to invest in a diversified portfolio. This chapter explores the benefits of mutual funds, such as professional management and diversification. It provides guidance on evaluating different types of funds, including equity, bond, index, balanced, and actively managed funds. It discusses expense ratios, load fees, and performance metrics to help readers make informed investment decisions when considering mutual funds.

In addition to mutual funds, readers are introduced to other pooled investment vehicles like hedge funds, private equity funds, and venture capital funds. This chapter overviews their unique characteristics, potential returns, and risks of such alternative investments. It explores the requirements and limitations of investing in these vehicles, ensuring readers understand all available investment options comprehensively.

Real estate investments have long been recognized as a tangible and potentially lucrative asset class. This chapter delves into the various forms of real estate investments, such as rental properties, real estate investment trusts (REITs), real estate crowdfunding, and real estate partnerships. It discusses the factors to consider when investing in real estate, such as location, market conditions, f i nancing options, and risk tolerance.

Moreover, this extended version explores real estate investment analysis, covering topics like property evaluation, cash ow projections, and determining the potential return on investment (ROI). It also delves into the complexities of property management and the importance of conducting thorough due diligence before making real estate investments.

Retirement planning is crucial to securing a comfortable future. Starting early and being aware of various retirement-saving options is crucial. This chapter explores employer-sponsored plans like 401(k)s, Roth IRAs, traditional IRAs, and SEP IRAs. It discusses contribution limits, tax advantages, and withdrawal rules while highlighting the importance of taking advantage of employer-matching contributions and maximizing tax-deferred growth.

Moreover, it explores alternative retirement savings options, such as Health Savings Accounts (HSAs) can provide a tax-advantaged way to save for medical expenses in retirement. This article explains the eligibility criteria and potential benefits of contributing to an HSA, including the ability to invest funds for potential growth.

This chapter also explores annuities, both immediate and deferred. It provides insights into how annuities work, the potential benefits of annuitizing retirement savings, and the considerations to keep in mind when considering annuities as part of a retirement plan.

This extended version delves further into the complexities of Social Security, providing insights on how to maximize benefits by understanding various claiming strategies, spousal bene ts, and strategies for divorced individuals. It also explains the potential impact of early or delayed claiming decisions and discusses provisions for survivors and individuals who have been unable to work due to disability.

Moreover, this chapter delves into the importance of projecting future expenses accurately, considering factors such as healthcare costs, inflation, and lifestyle choices. It explores strategies to manage asset allocation and withdrawal rates during retirement, ensuring sustainable income throughout one's later years.

Estate planning is often overlooked but is a crucial aspect of planning for the future. In this extended version, we go deeper into all facets of estate planning to ensure readers have a comprehensive understanding. It starts with the importance of creating a will, detailing the necessary components and the potential consequences of not having one. This chapter also explores the benefits and complexities of trusts, such as revocable living trusts, irrevocable trusts, and special needs trusts. It provides insights into naming trustees, successor trustees, and trust protectors to ensure proper management of assets.

Moreover, it delves into the significance of naming beneficiaries and contingent beneficiaries for various assets, including life insurance policies, retirement accounts, and investment accounts. By doing so, readers can ensure that their assets are distributed according to their wishes while minimizing potential costs and delays.

Tax considerations are an integral part of estate planning. This chapter provides insights into estate and inheritance taxes, discussing strategies to minimize tax liabilities and protect wealth. It delves into strategies like gifting, charitable giving, and family limited partnerships, enabling readers to develop tax-efficient estate plans. It also emphasizes the importance of regularly reviewing and updating estate planning documents to reflect any life changes, such as marriage, divorce, births, or deaths.

In addition to the practicalities of estate planning, this extended chapter explores the emotional aspects involved. It delves into the importance of open and honest communication with loved ones regarding end-of-life wishes, medical directives, and the appointment of a healthcare proxy or power of attorney. It discusses the benefits of involving professionals, such as financial advisors, estate planners, attorneys, and accountants, to ensure a comprehensive and effective plan.

By engaging in effective investment strategies, creating a robust retirement plan, and undertaking thorough estate planning, individuals and couples can achieve financial security while safeguarding their legacies. This extended chapter empowers readers to take control of their financial futures, providing them with an in-depth understanding of the various investment options, retirement planning strategies, and estate planning essentials.

Armed with this knowledge, readers can make informed decisions to secure a prosperous future for themselves and their loved ones.

Conclusion

As we reach the final chapter of this transformative book, it is crucial to delve even deeper into the intricacies of financial inequality within relationships. Throughout these pages, we have explored the multifaceted nature of this issue, dissecting its origins, impact, and potential solutions. We have delved into the underlying power dynamics, societal norms, and personal biases that contribute to this pervasive problem.

financial inequality within relationships is not a standalone issue but rather intimately intertwined with the broader socio-economic fabric of society. It is deeply influenced by systemic factors such as wage gaps, employment opportunities, and access to resources and education. These issues disproportionally affect marginalized communities, exacerbating the already existing gaps in financial equality. Understanding the intersectionality of financial inequality is crucial to addressing it effectively.

While the concept of financial inequality may seem straightforward on the surface, it encompasses far more than the disparity in income or wealth between partners. It also encompasses unresolved emotional baggage, differing financial philosophies, and ingrained gender roles. These underlying dynamics can create a complex web that entangles couples in a cycle of inequality, hindering their ability to achieve financial parity.

To truly address financial inequality, we must confront the societal expectations and cultural norms that perpetuate it. Traditional gender roles, often reinforced by media and societal narratives, have long assigned men as the primary breadwinners, while women have been expected to take on caregiving roles. These predefined roles not only limit individual choices but also create an environment where financial power is concentrated within a single partner, leading to imbalances in decision-making and perpetuating disempowerment for the other.

Moreover, the impact of financial inequality extends beyond the immediate relationship dynamics. It ripples out into wider social and economic disparities, affecting individuals' mental health, self-esteem, and overall well-being. Financial stress can lead to strained relationships, decreased productivity, and increased susceptibility to mental health issues. It is a multifaceted problem that demands comprehensive solutions.

Constructing a foundation of open and honest communication is paramount to overcoming financial inequality within relationships. Couples must create a safe space where financial matters can be brought to the forefront without fear of judgment or ego. Initiating these conversations can be uncomfortable, as it requires vulnerability and trust. However, this willingness to confront and address financial concerns is an essential step towards cultivating equality.

During these discussions, it is crucial to approach the topic with empathy and understanding. Recognizing that financial insecurity can trigger deep-seated emotions and insecurities is vital. Cultivating empathy lays the groundwork for mutual support, respect, and the ability to grow together rather than growing apart.

Education and empowerment are pivotal steps towards achieving financial equality within relationships. It is imperative for individuals within a partnership to actively seek knowledge to build their financial literacy. This includes understanding not only investment strategies, debt management, and financial planning techniques but also the structural factors influencing financial inequality. By obtaining a broader understanding of the system and actively challenging it, individuals can become advocates for change within their relationships and communities.

Furthermore, financial independence is a goal that should be pursued by all partners within a relationship. Striving to create a sense of self-sufficiency fosters a healthy dynamic built on mutual respect and interdependence. It ensures that both partners have a secure foundation and the ability to contribute meaningfully to the relationship's financial well-being. Financial independence grants individuals agency and the freedom to pursue their passions, dreams, and career goals, making the relationship an equal partnership of shared responsibility.

In addition to financial independence, recognizing and celebrating the unique qualities and contributions each partner brings to the relationship is vital. It is essential to acknowledge that financial power does not de ne an individual's worth or the value they bring to the partnership. Each person possesses talents, skills, and personal qualities that enhance the dynamics of the relationship in numerous ways. By embracing and celebrating these differences, couples can foster an environment of synergistic collaboration, where financial power does not overshadow other aspects of their connection.

Lastly, it is crucial to remember that change takes time and patience. Overcoming financial inequality is not an overnight process but a long-term commitment requiring ongoing effort and dedication from both partners. Obstacles and setbacks may occur along the way, but they should be seen as opportunities for growth and learning rather than as failures. By embracing these challenges as catalysts for personal and relational growth, couples can continue to progress towards a relationship rooted in equality, trust, and collaboration.

In conclusion, as you embark on your journey towards financial equality, let these principles guide you. Delve deep into the roots of financial inequality, challenging societal norms that perpetuate it. Foster open and honest communication, creating an environment of understanding and respect. Empower yourself with knowledge, striving for financial independence and advocating for change. Celebrate the unique strengths each partner brings to the relationship, recognizing their value beyond their financial contributions. And remember, progress takes time, patience, and compassion. Through these efforts, you will forge a path towards a relationship grounded in equality, where both partners can thrive and flourish.

www.ingramcontent.com/pod-product-compliance
Lightning Source LLC
LaVergne TN
LVHW022027200926
848481LV00007B/2580
* 9 7 9 8 3 4 8 5 6 5 7 0 1 *